Eight Opera Themes

Transcribed and arranged for

Two Guitars and Bb Clarinet / Flute

1. Largo al factotum from "Il barbiere di Siviglia" by G. Rossini

Score p. 3, Bb Clarinet p. 9, Guitar 1 p. 12, Guitar 2 p. 15, Flute p. 71

2. Non più andrai from "Le nozze di Figaro" by W.A. Mozart

Score p. 18, Bb Clarinet p. 21, Guitar 1 p. 23, Guitar 2 p. 25, Flute p. 74

3. Deh vieni alla finestra from "Don Giovanni" by W.A. Mozart

Score p. 27, Bb Clarinet p. 30, Guitar 1 p. 31, Guitar 2 p. 33, Flute p. 76

4. Là ci darem la mano from "Don Giovanni" by W.A. Mozart

Score p. 35, Bb Clarinet p. 37, Guitar 1 p. 38, Guitar 2 p. 39, Flute p. 77

5. Se il mio nome saper voi bramate from "Il barbiere di Siviglia" by G. Rossini

Score p. 40, Bb Clarinet p. 42, Guitars 1 and 2 p. 43, Flute p. 78

6. E lucevan le stelle from "Tosca" by G. Puccini

Score p. 45, Bb Clarinet p. 48, Guitars 1 and 2 p. 51, Flute p. 79

7. Queen of the night's aria from "The magic flute" by W.A. Mozart

Score p. 53, Bb Clarinet p. 57, Guitar 1 p. 59, Guitar 2 p. 61, Flute p. 82

8. Nessun dorma from "Tourandot" by G. Puccini

Score p. 63, Bb Clarinet p. 66, Guitars 1 and 2 p. 68, Flute p. 84

All themes by respective composers and owners, transcription arranged for 2 guitars and Bb Clarinet / Flute made by Antonio Zaccaria in 2015. Cover artwork and painting by Svetlana Kartashova (Sveta Skripka) in 2015.

Visit www.AntonioZaccaria.com

Hi this is Antonio, I'd like to thank you for the interest in this work of mine. The transcriptions were made for my music students to give them some nice and famous themes to work and practice with. The guitar arrangements are often separated in two different parts that will complete each other while some transcription is written in an unique part intended to be played at unison by the two guitarists. The clarinet parts often come with written dinamics and phrase indications while some can be interpreted freely instead. My primary target was to create enjoyable music for an uncommon chamber ensemble, guitar and Bb Clarinet: as a matter of fact, there is a little repertoire written for this formation. At the end of the book you will find all the clarinet parts transcribed for flute, in order to let other musicians read and play the themes in a standard notation. I hope you will enjoy playing my transcriptions and please visit my website at **www.AntonioZaccaria.com** to contact me and know more about my guitarist and teacher career.

Largo al factotum

Theme from "Il barbiere di Siviglia" by G. Rossini - 1816

Transcription and arrangement by Antonio Zaccaria - 2015

Largo al factotum

Theme from "Il barbiere di Siviglia" by G. Rossini - 1816

Transcription and arrangement by Antonio Zaccaria - 2015

10

Largo al factotum

Theme from "Il barbiere di Siviglia" by G. Rossini - 1816

Transcription and arrangement by Antonio Zaccaria - 2015

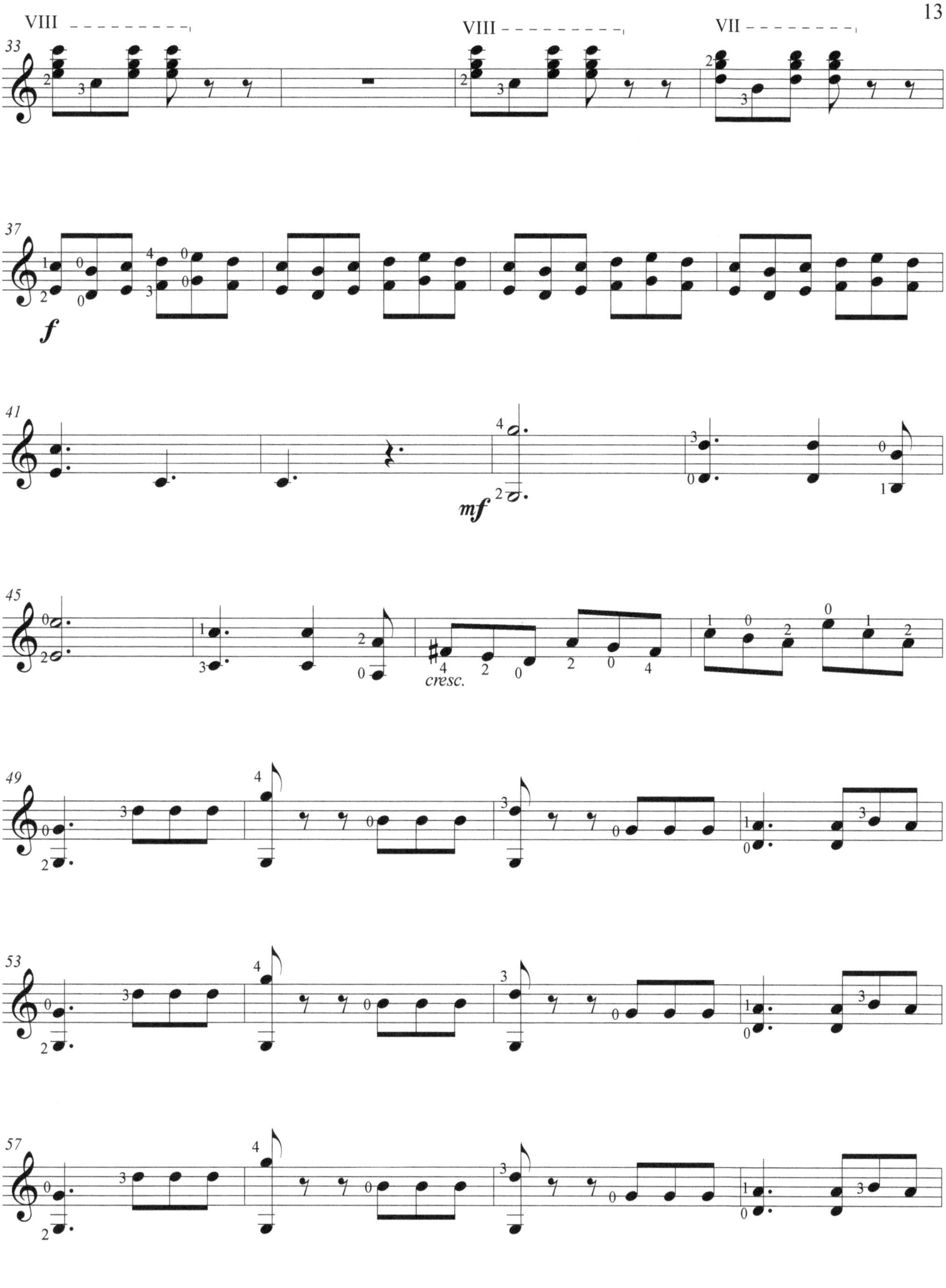
VIII
VIII
VII
f
mf
cresc.
cresc.

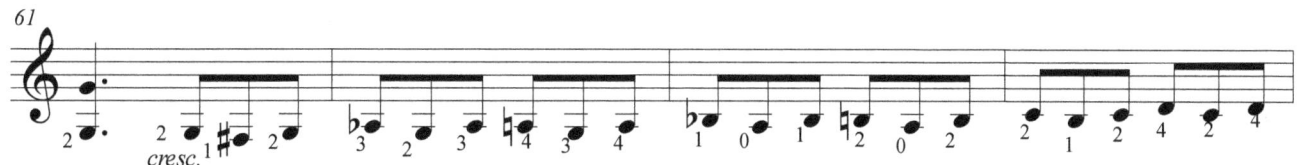

Largo al factotum

Theme from "Il barbiere di Siviglia" by G. Rossini - 1816

Transcription and arrangement by Antonio Zaccaria - 2015

Non più andrai

Theme from "Le nozze di Figaro" by W. A. Mozart - 1786

Transcription and arrangement by Antonio Zaccaria - 2015

19

Non più andrai

Theme from "Le nozze di Figaro" by W. A. Mozart - 1786

Transcription and arrangement by Antonio Zaccaria - 2015

Non più andrai

Theme from "Le nozze di Figaro" by W. A. Mozart - 1786

Transcription and arrangement by Antonio Zaccaria - 2015

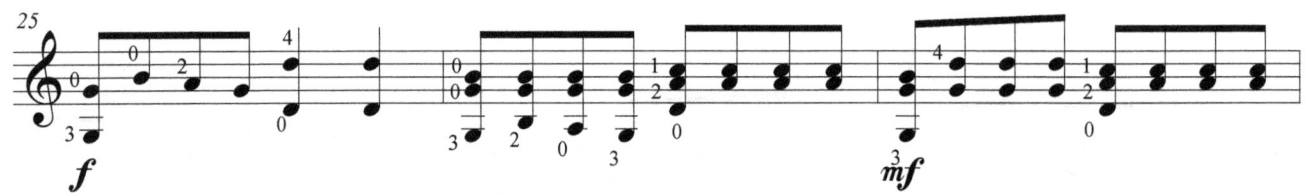
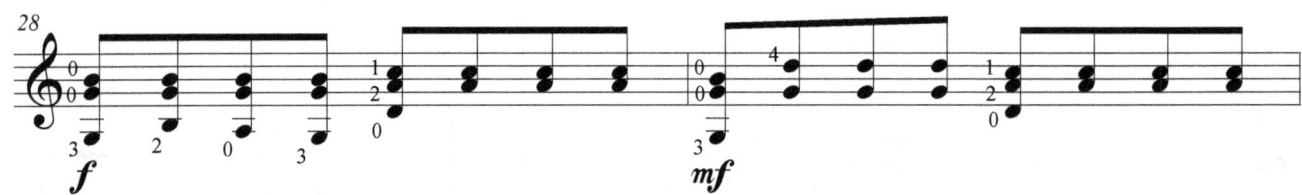
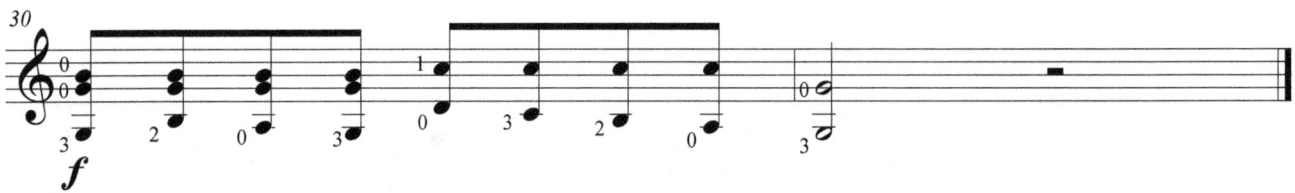

Non più andrai

Theme from "Le nozze di Figaro" by W. A. Mozart - 1786

Transcription and arrangement by Antonio Zaccaria - 2015

Deh vieni alla finestra

Theme from "Don Giovanni" by W.A. Mozart - 1787

Transcription and arrangement by Antonio Zaccaria - 2015

Deh vieni alla finestra

Theme from "Don Giovanni" by W.A. Mozart - 1787

Transcription and arrangement by Antonio Zaccaria - 2015

Deh vieni alla finestra

Theme from "Don Giovanni" by W.A. Mozart - 1787

Transcription and arrangement by Antonio Zaccaria - 2015

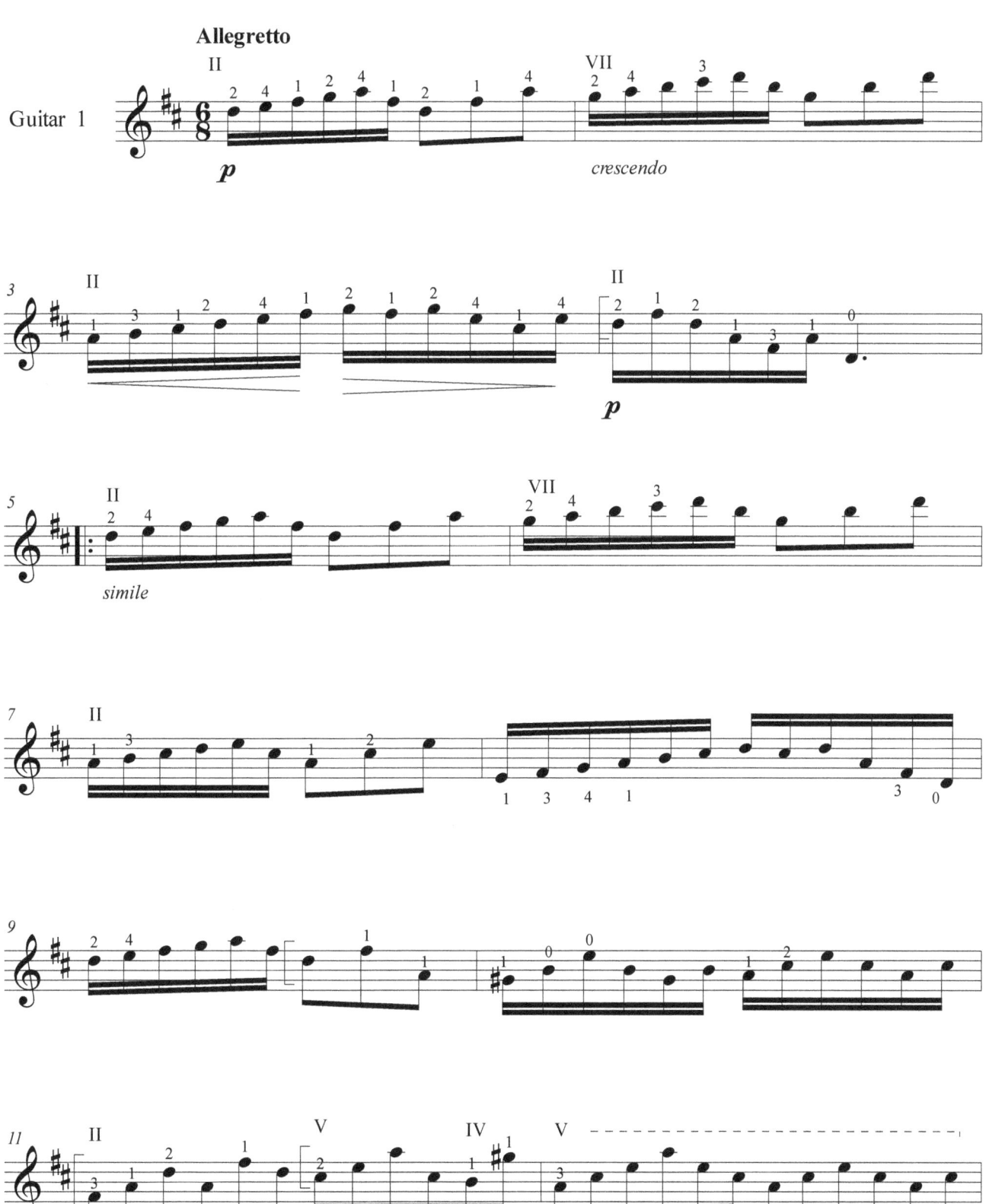

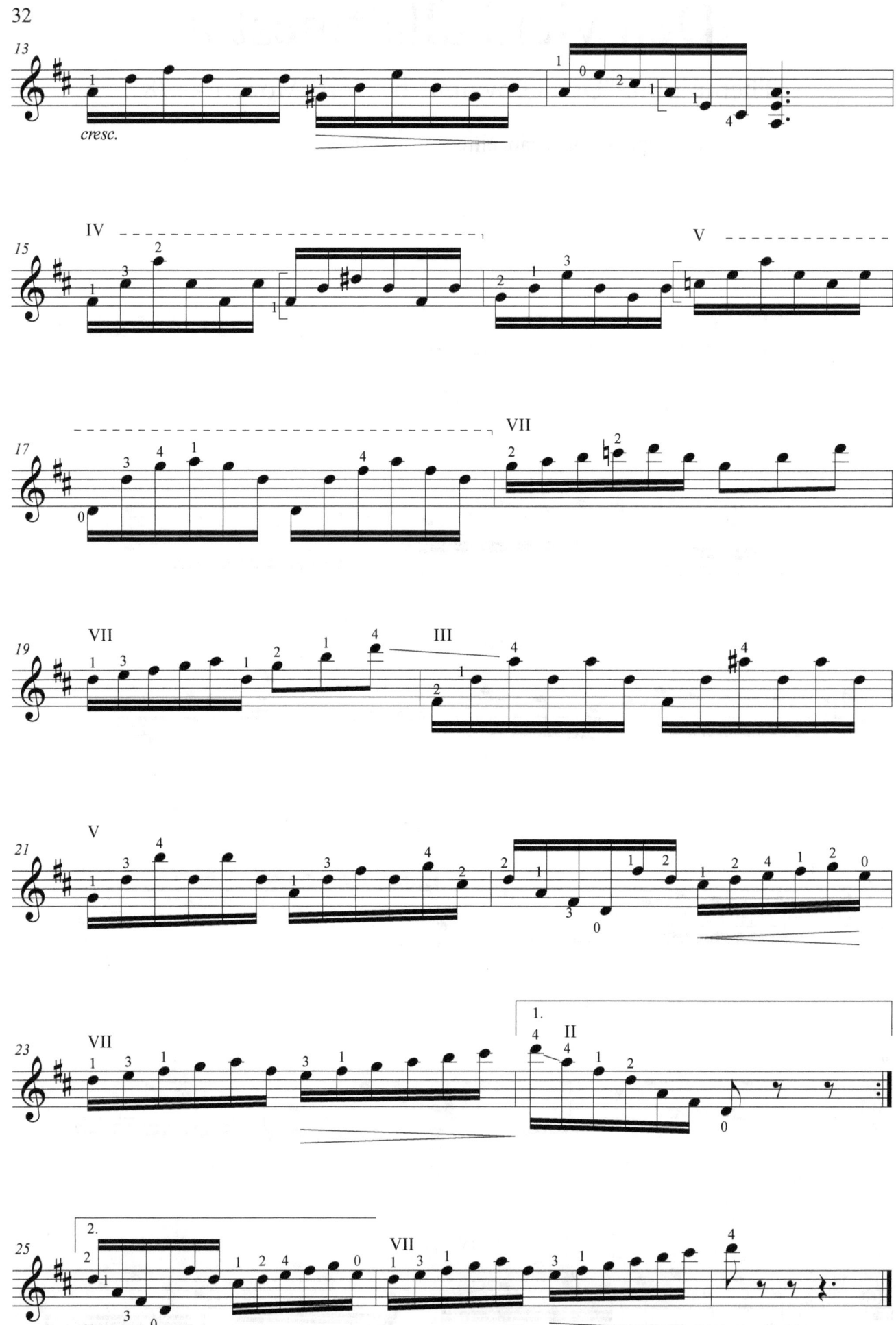

Deh vieni alla finestra

Theme from "Don Giovanni" by W.A. Mozart - 1787

Transcription and arrangement by Antonio Zaccaria - 2015

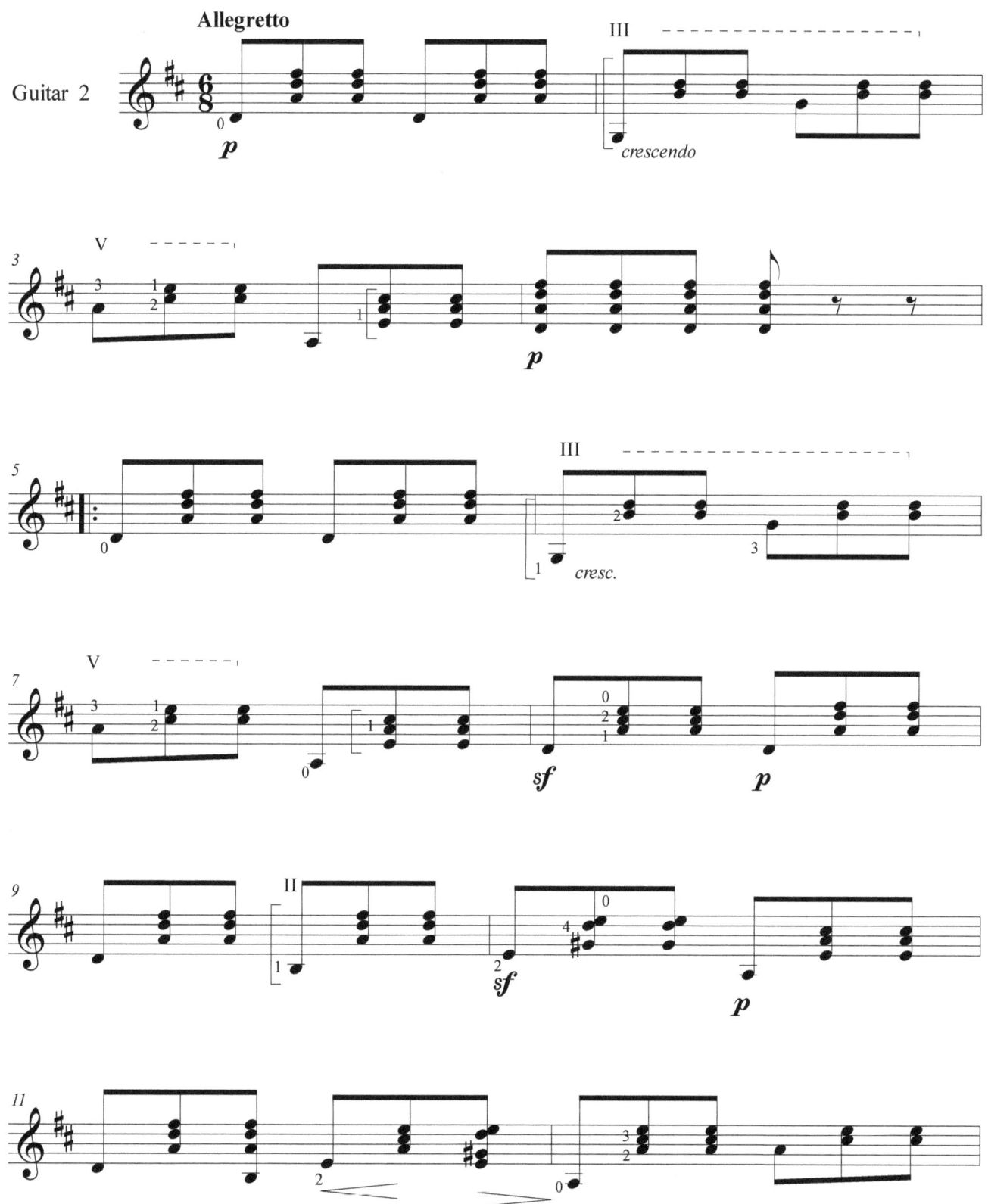

Là ci darem la mano

Theme from "Don Giovanni" by W.A. Mozart - 1787

Transcription and arrangement by Antonio Zaccaria - 2015

Segue "Se il mio nome saper voi bramate"

Là ci darem la mano

Theme from "Don Giovanni" by W.A. Mozart - 1787

Transcription and arrangement by Antonio Zaccaria - 2015

Segue "Se il mio nome saper voi bramate"

Là ci darem la mano

Theme from "Don Giovanni" by W.A. Mozart - 1787

Transcription and arrangement by Antonio Zaccaria - 2015

Segue "Se il mio nome saper voi bramate"

Là ci darem la mano

Theme from "Don Giovanni" by W.A. Mozart - 1787

Transcription and arrangement by Antonio Zaccaria - 2015

Segue "Se il mio nome saper voi bramate"

Se il mio nome saper voi bramate

Theme from "Il barbiere di Siviglia" by G. Rossini - 1816

Transcription and arrangement by Antonio Zaccaria - 2015

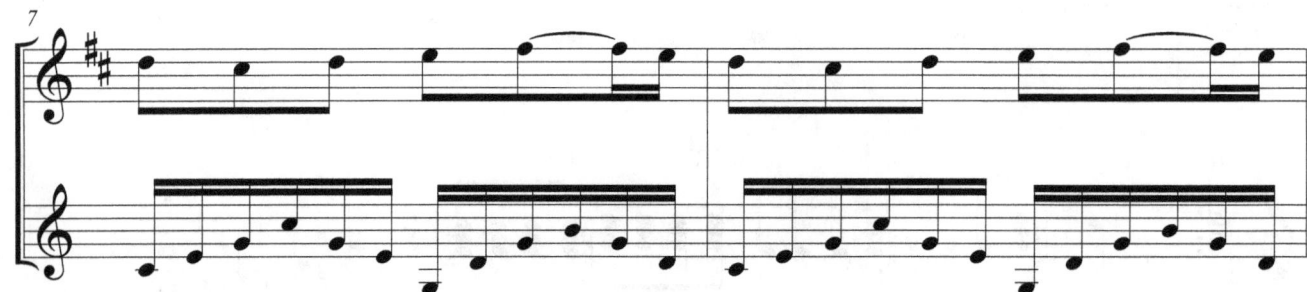

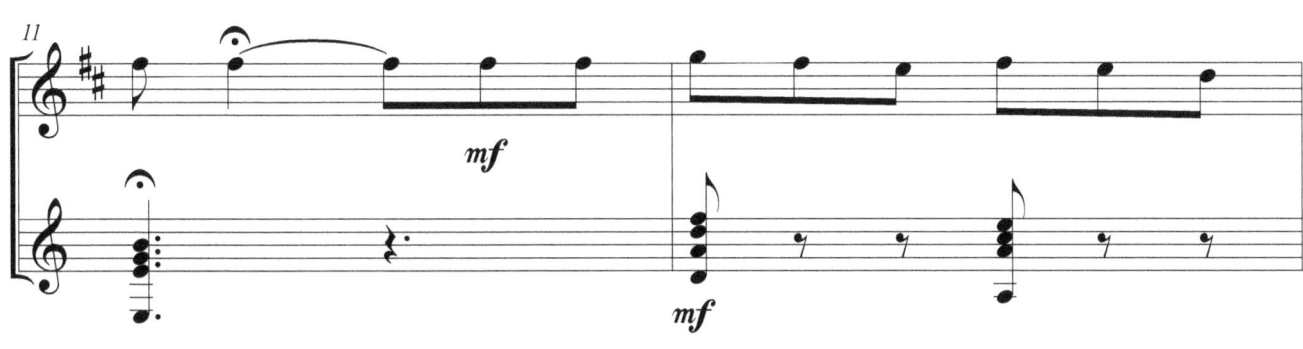
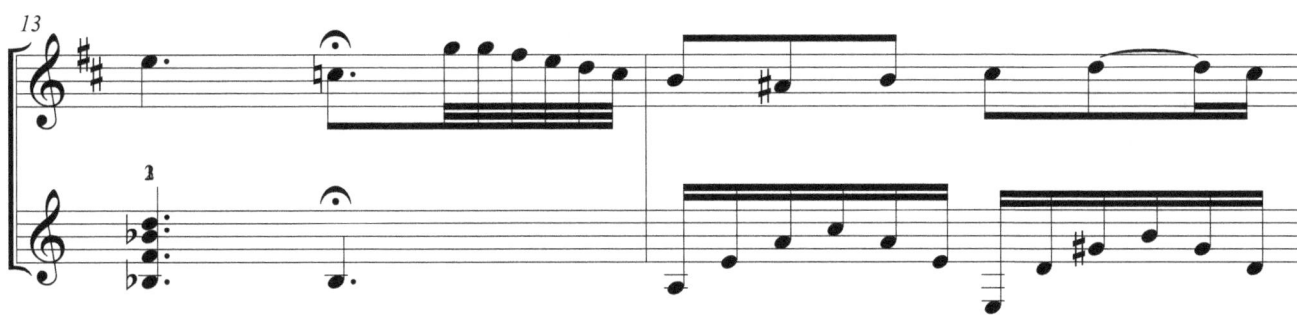

Se il mio nome saper voi bramate

Theme from "Il barbiere di Siviglia" by G. Rossini - 1816

Transcription and arrangement by Antonio Zaccaria - 2015

Se il mio nome saper voi bramate

Theme from "Il barbiere di Siviglia" by G. Rossini - 1816

Transcription and arrangement by Antonio Zaccaria - 2015

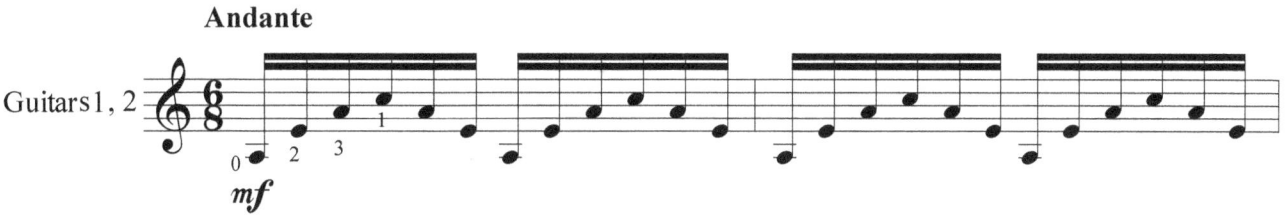

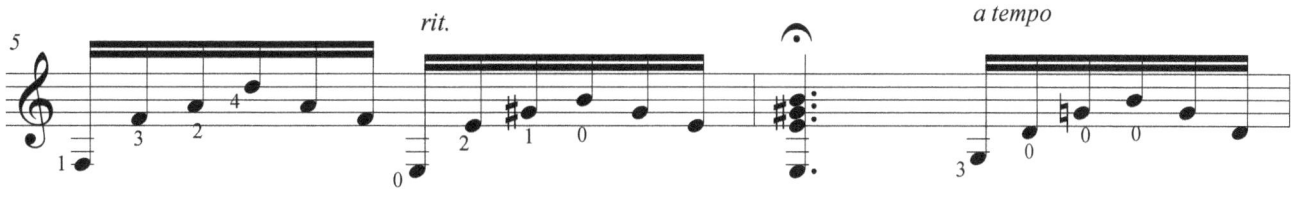

E lucevan le stelle

Theme from "Tosca" by G. Puccini - 1900

Transcription and arrangement by Antonio Zaccaria - 2015

E lucevan le stelle

Theme from "Tosca" by G. Puccini - 1900

Transcription and arrangement by Antonio Zaccaria - 2015

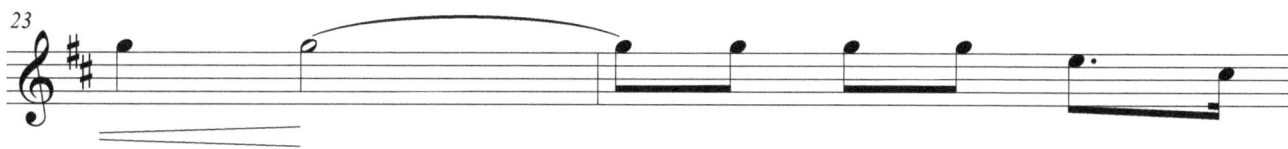

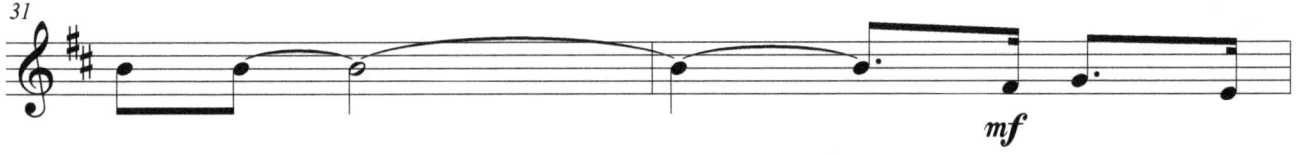

E lucevan le stelle

Theme from "Tosca" by G. Puccini - 1900

Transcription and arrangement by Antonio Zaccaria - 2015

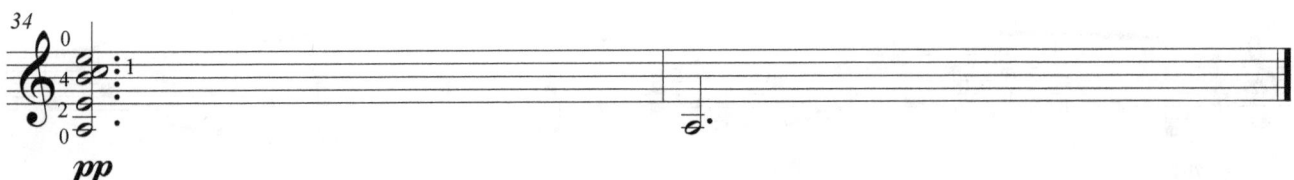

Queen of the Night's Aria

Theme from "The Magic Flute" by W. A. Mozart - 1791

Transcription and arrangement by Antonio Zaccaria - 2015

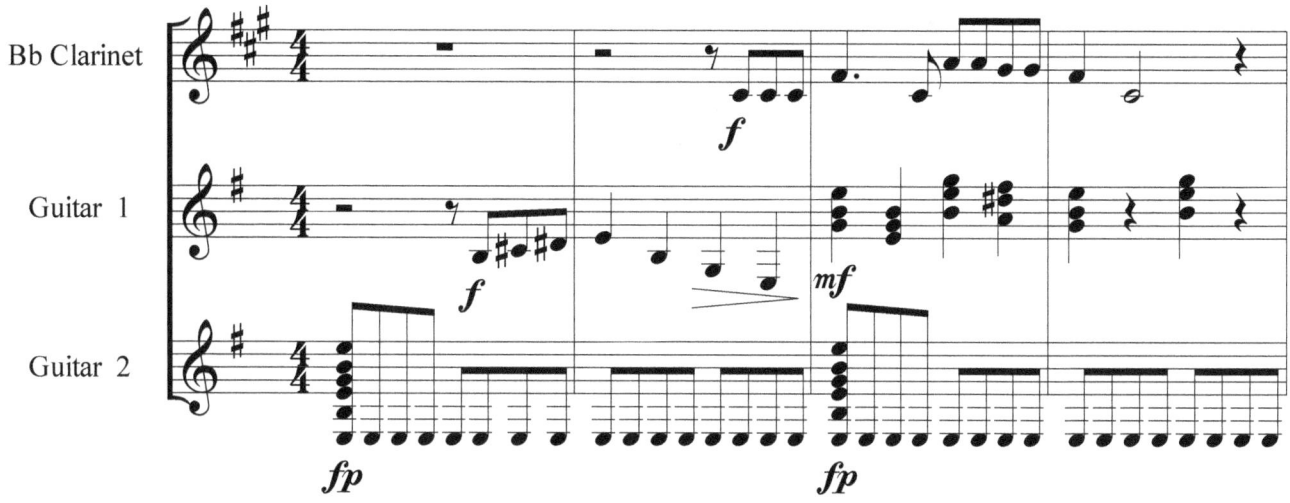

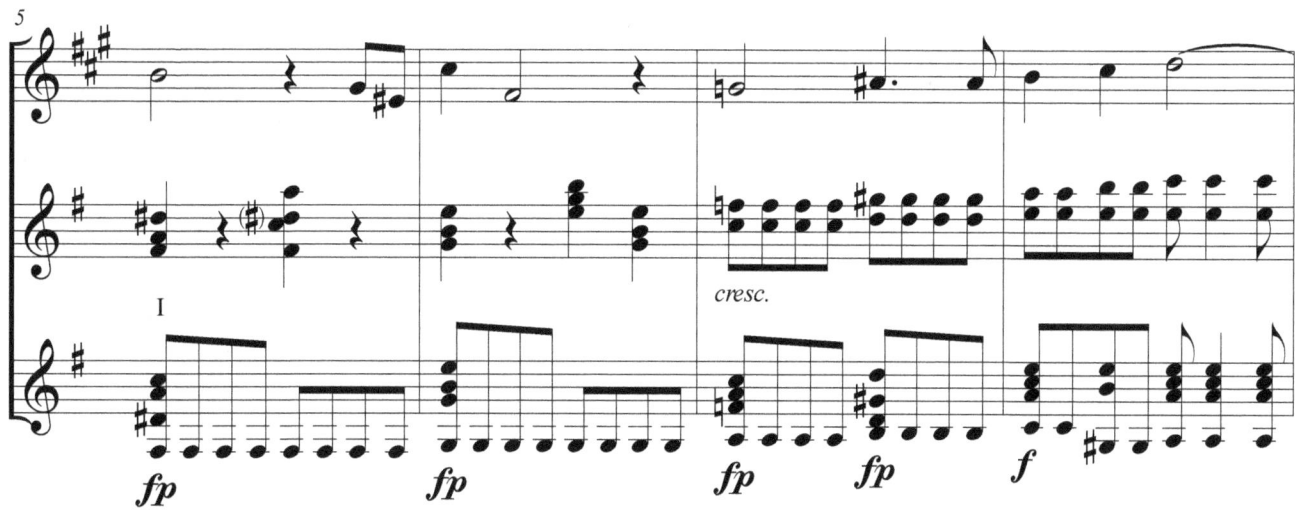

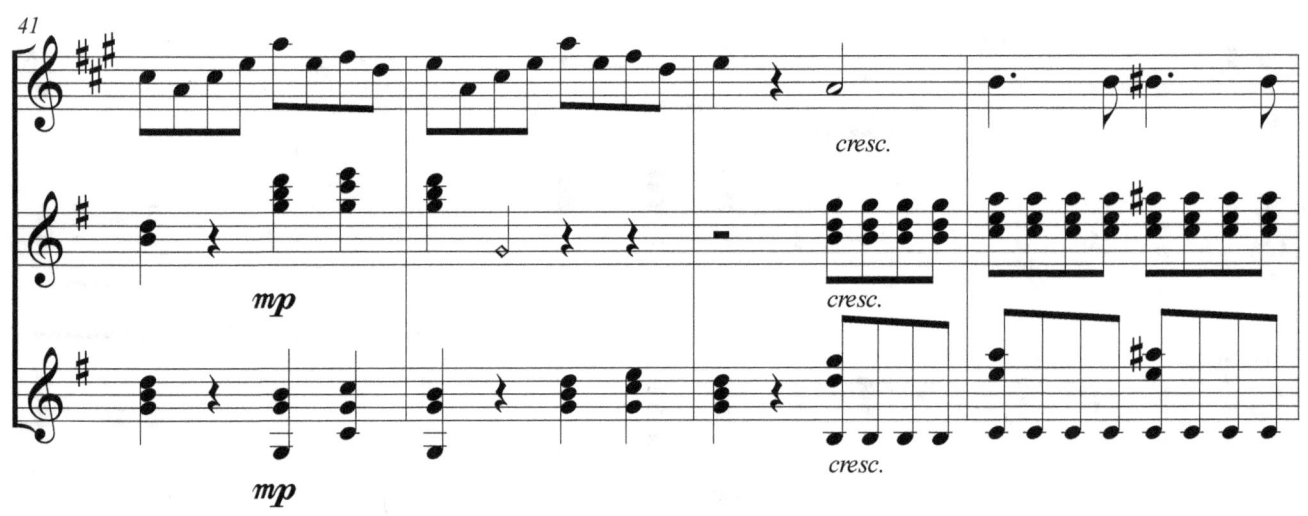

Queen of the Night's Aria

Theme from "The Magic Flute" by W. A. Mozart - 1791

Transcription and arrangement by Antonio Zaccaria - 2015

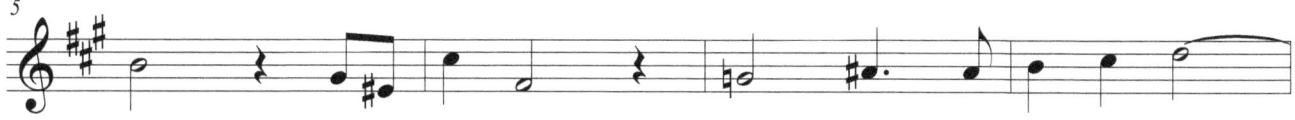
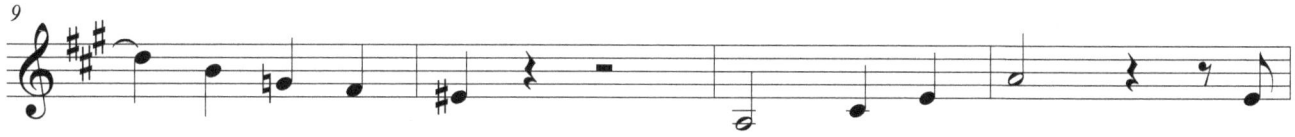

Queen of the Night's Aria

Theme from "The Magic Flute" by W. A. Mozart - 1791

Transcription and arrangement by Antonio Zaccaria - 2015

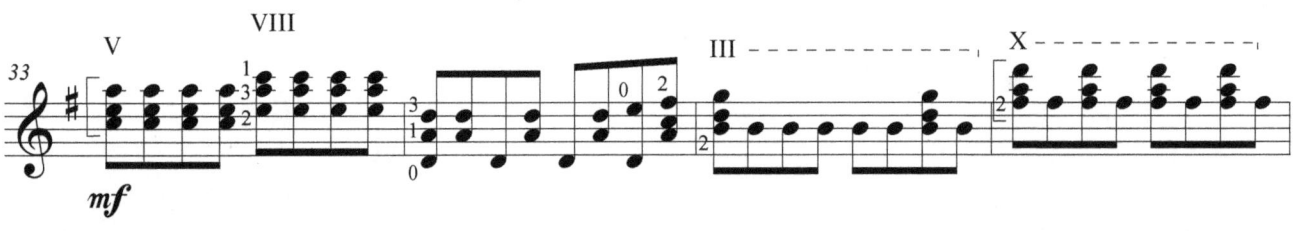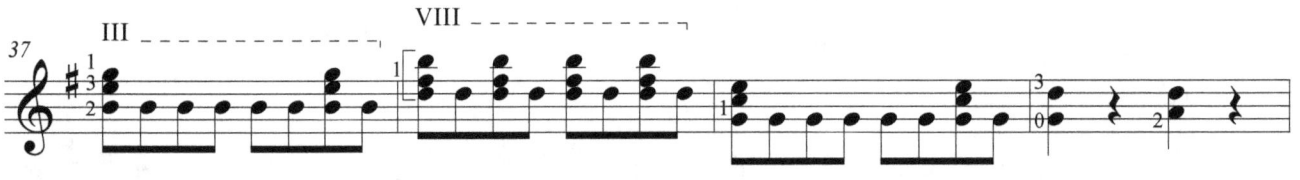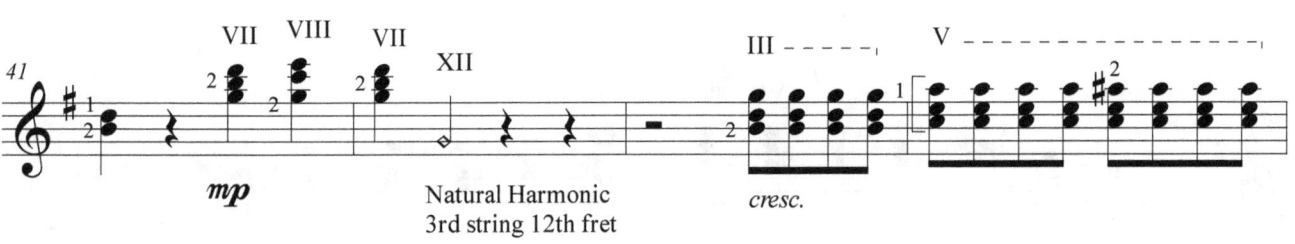

Queen of the Night's Aria

Theme from "The Magic Flute" by W. A. Mozart - 1791

Transcription and arrangement by Antonio Zaccaria - 2015

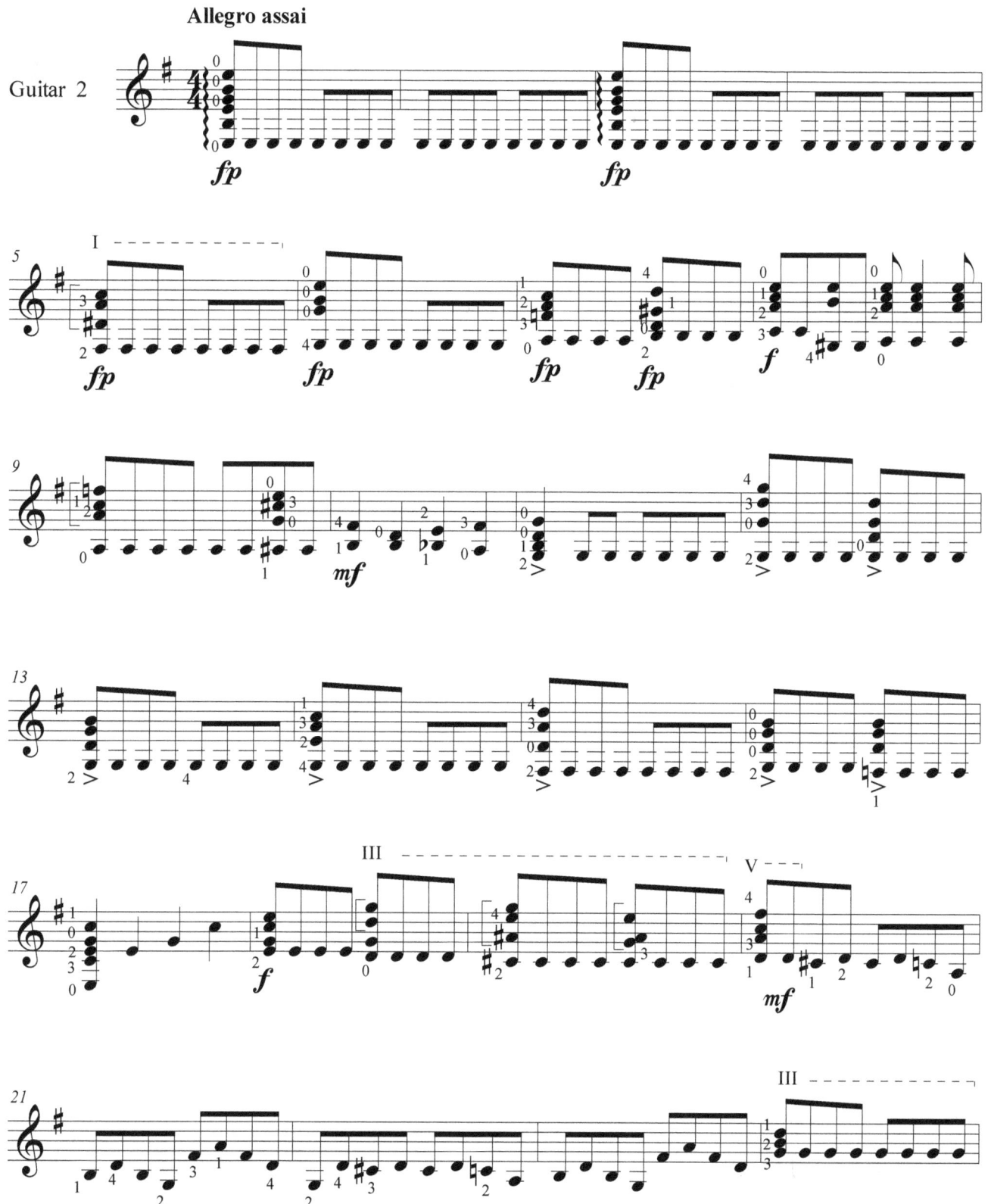

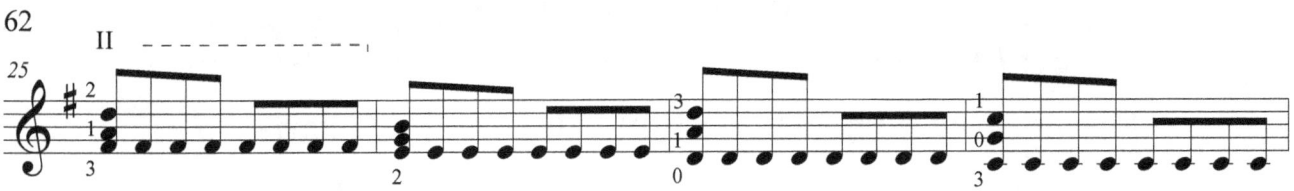
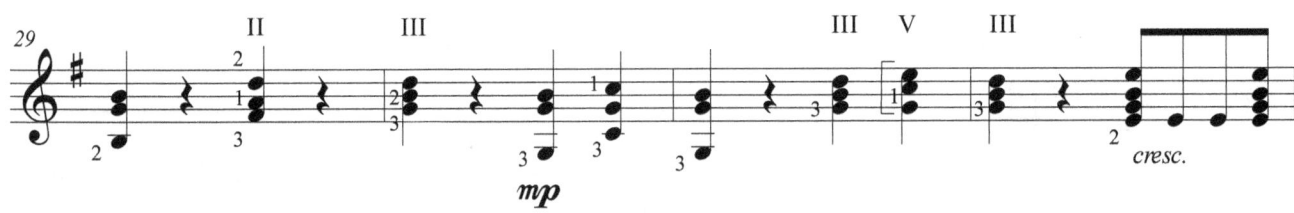
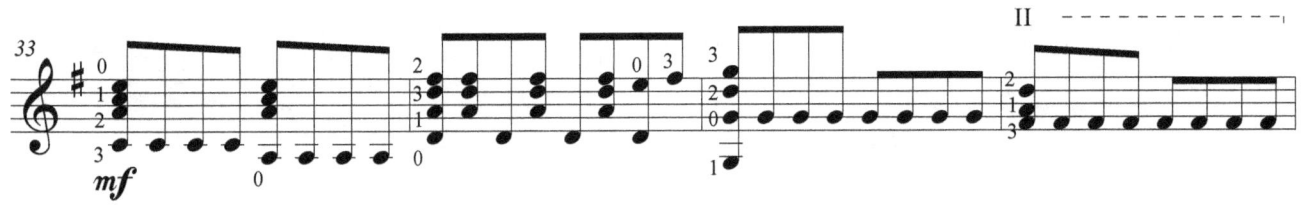

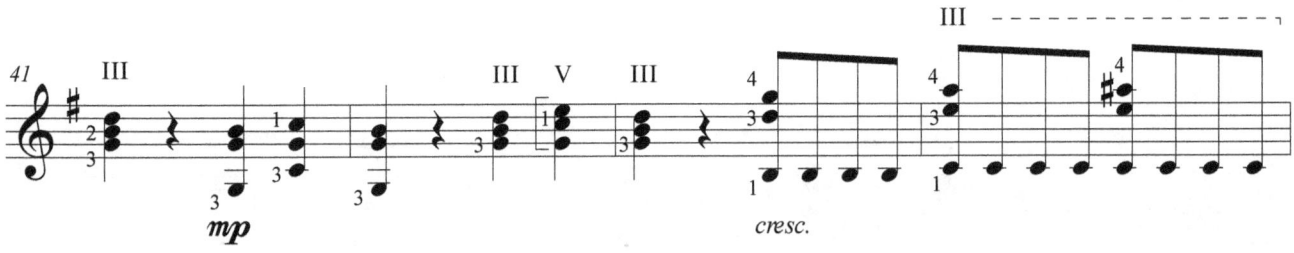
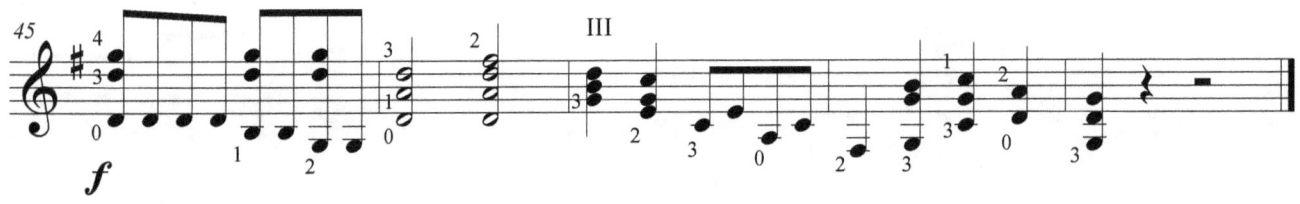

Nessun dorma

Theme form "Turandot" by G. Puccini - 1926

Transcription and arrangement by Antonio Zaccaria - 2015

The guitars perform tremolo technique, here is notated in a simpler way for practical needs.

Nessun dorma

Theme form "Turandot" by G. Puccini - 1926

Transcription and arrangement by Antonio Zaccaria - 2015

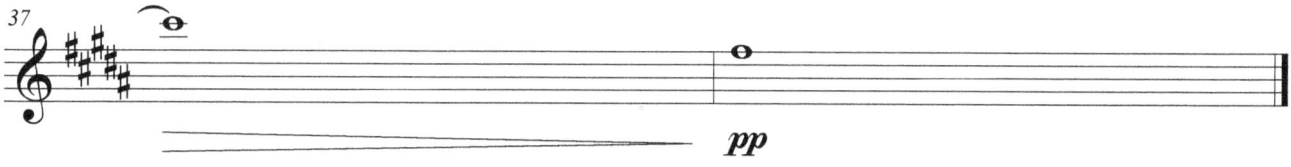

Nessun dorma

Theme form "Turandot" by G. Puccini - 1926

Transcription and arrangement by Antonio Zaccaria - 2015

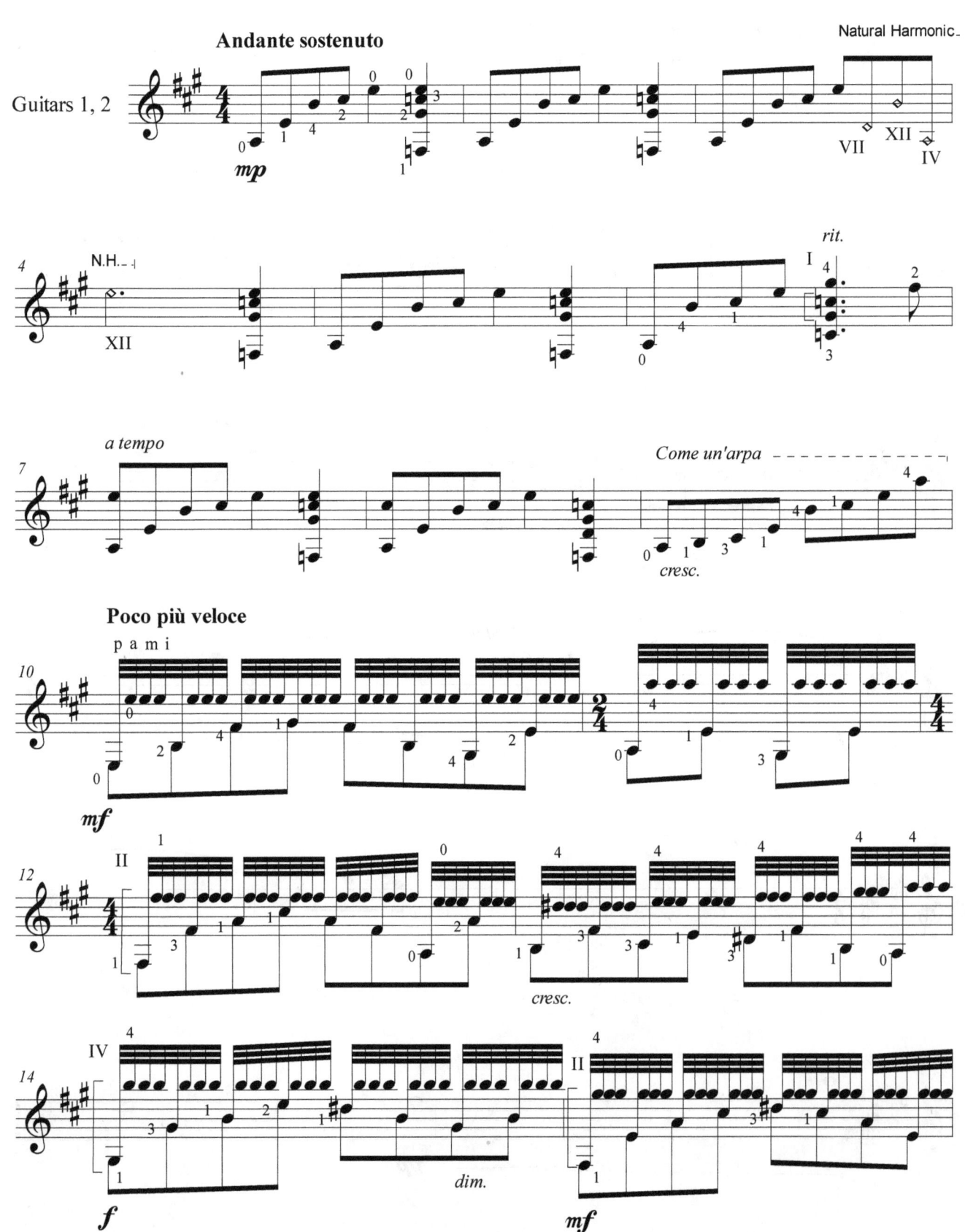

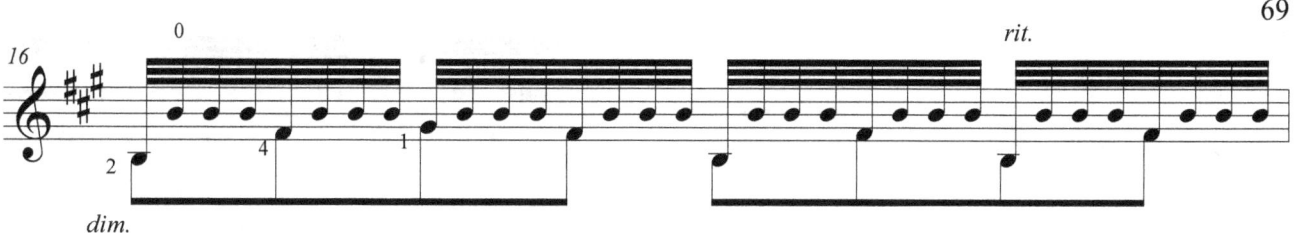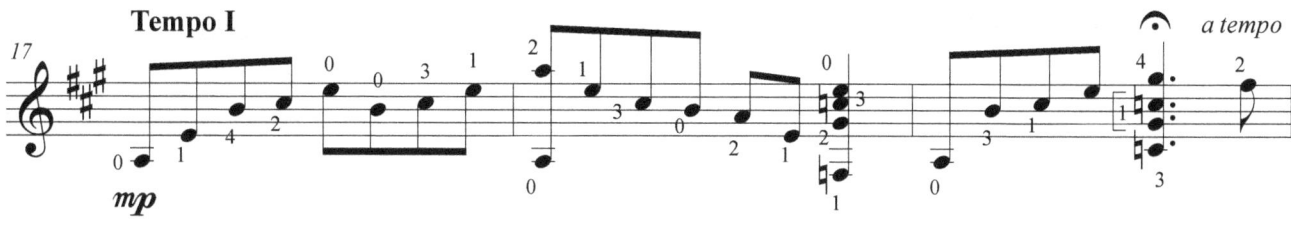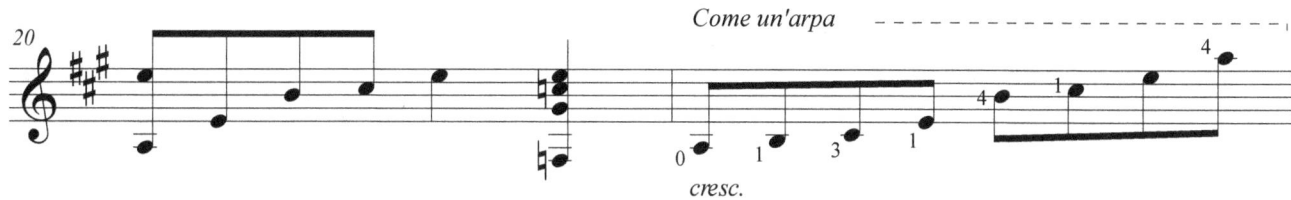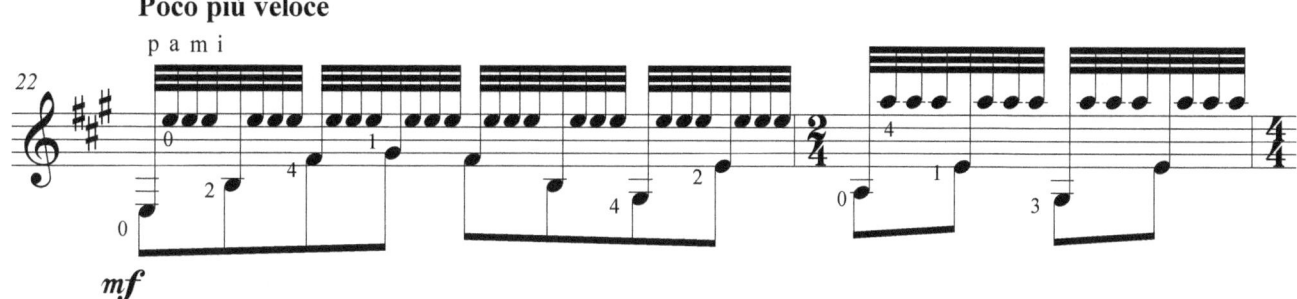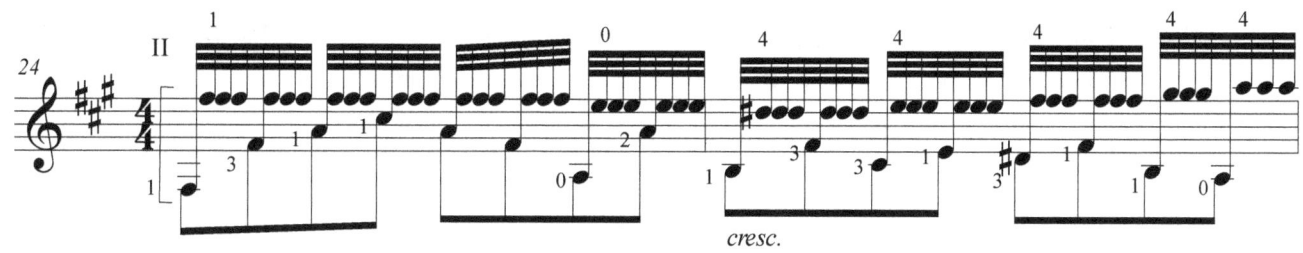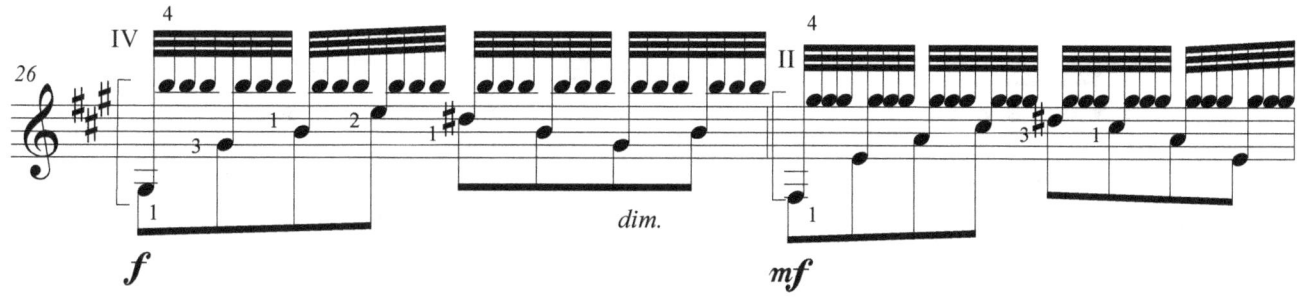

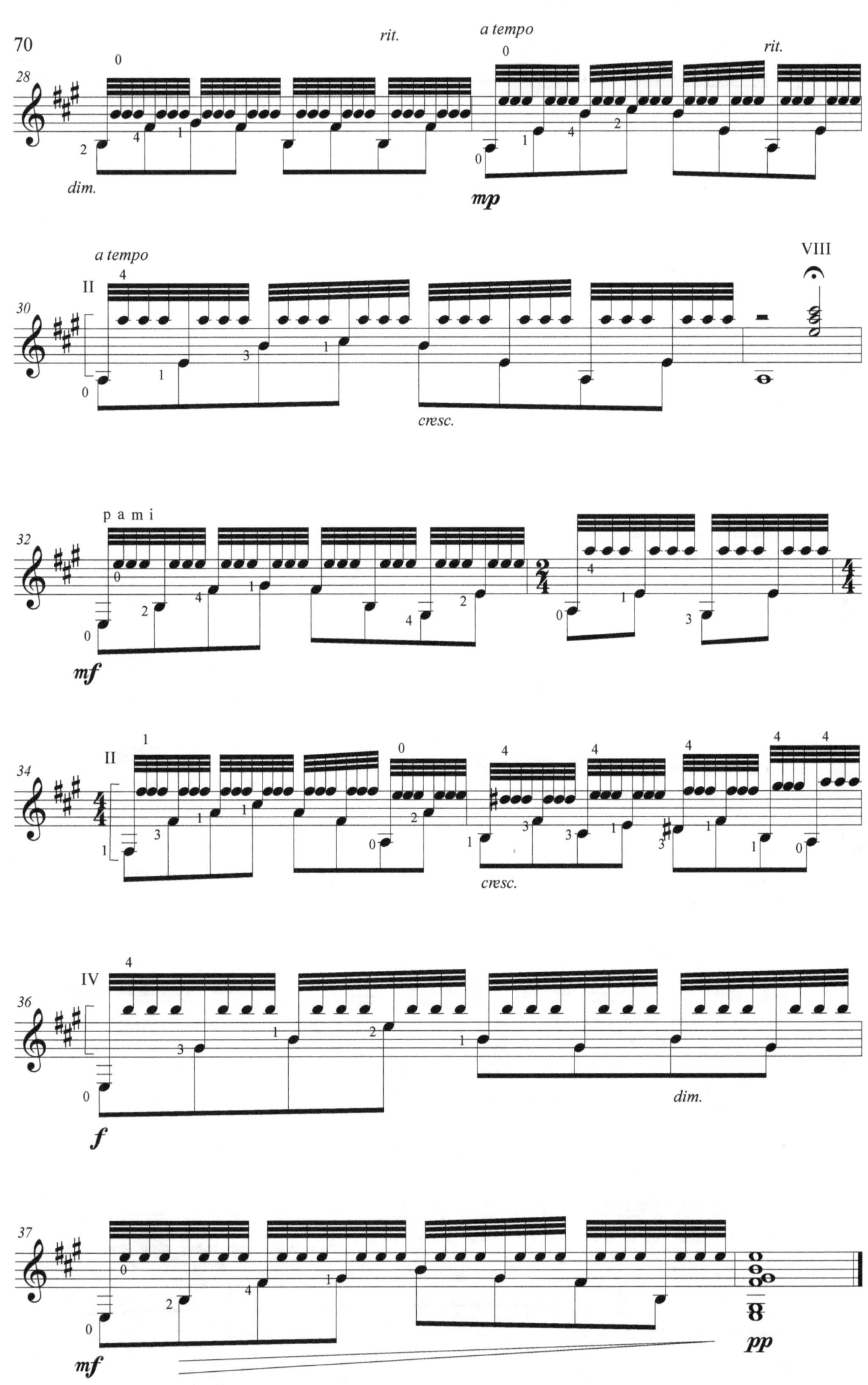

Largo al factotum

Theme from "Il barbiere di Siviglia" by G. Rossini - 1816

Transcription and arrangement by Antonio Zaccaria - 2015

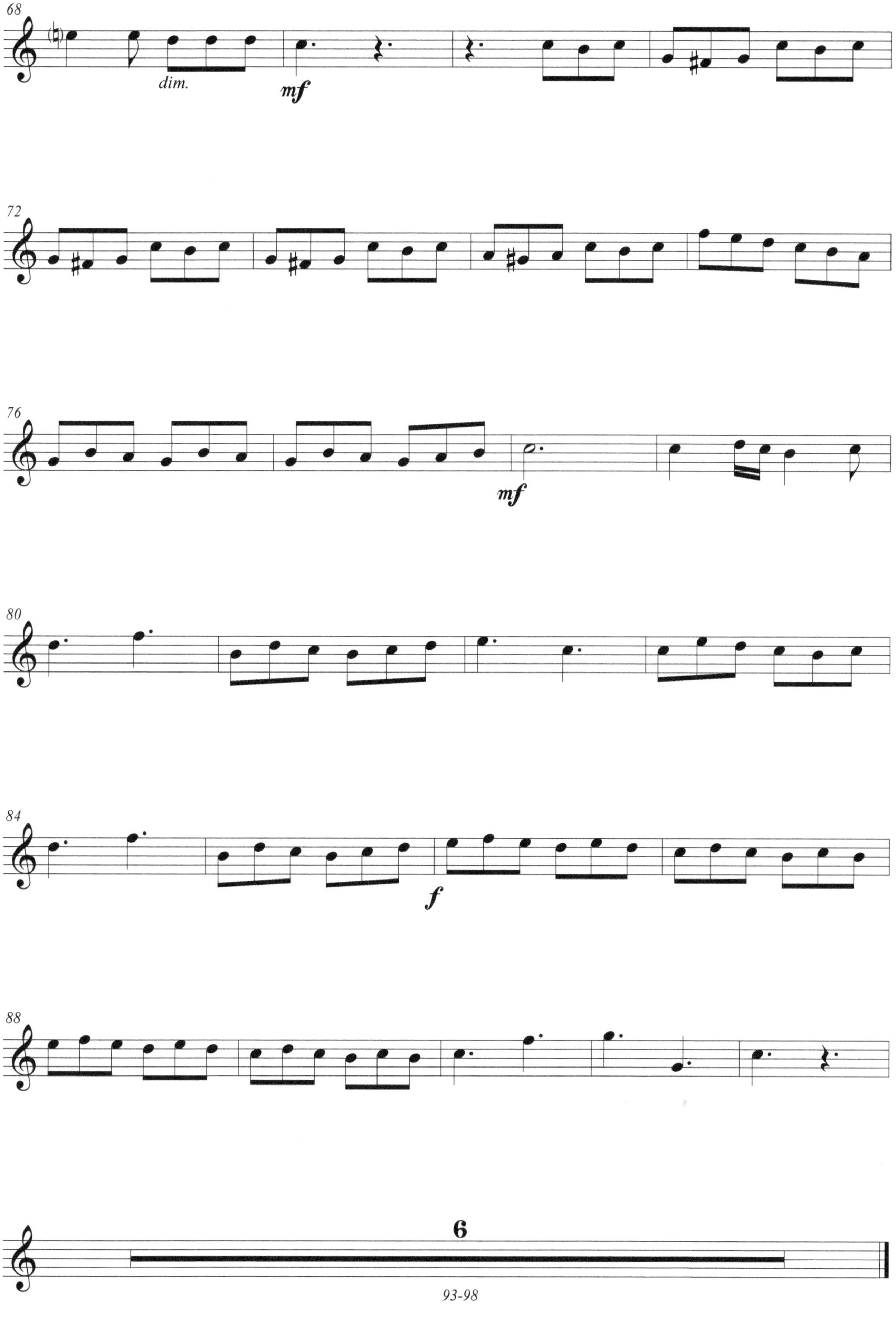
68
dim.
mf
72
76
mf
80
84
f
88
6
93-98

Non più andrai

Theme from "Le nozze di Figaro" by W. A. Mozart - 1786

Transcription and arrangement by Antonio Zaccaria - 2015

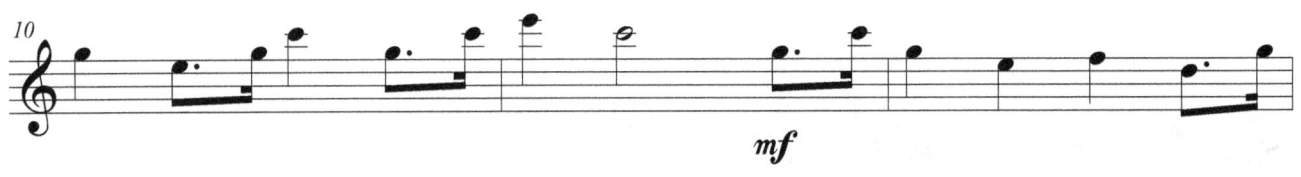

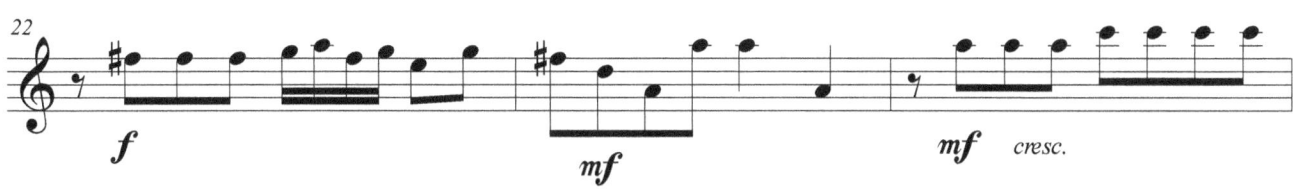

Deh vieni alla finestra

Theme from "Don Giovanni" by W.A. Mozart - 1787

Transcription and arrangement by Antonio Zaccaria - 2015

Là ci darem la mano

Theme from "Don Giovanni" by W.A. Mozart - 1787

Transcription and arrangement by Antonio Zaccaria - 2015

Segue "Se il mio nome saper voi bramate"

Se il mio nome saper voi bramate

Theme from "Il barbiere di Siviglia" by G. Rossini - 1816

Transcription and arrangement by Antonio Zaccaria - 2015

E lucevan le stelle

Theme from "Tosca" by G. Puccini - 1900

Transcription and arrangement by Antonio Zaccaria - 2015

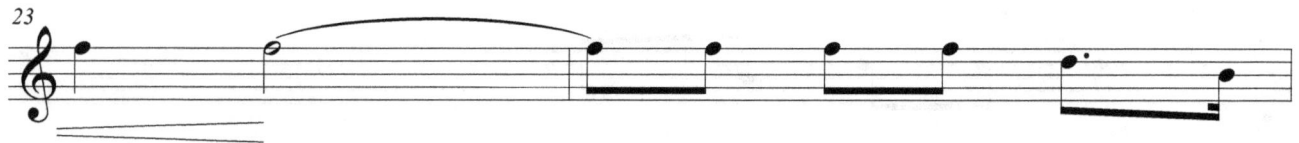

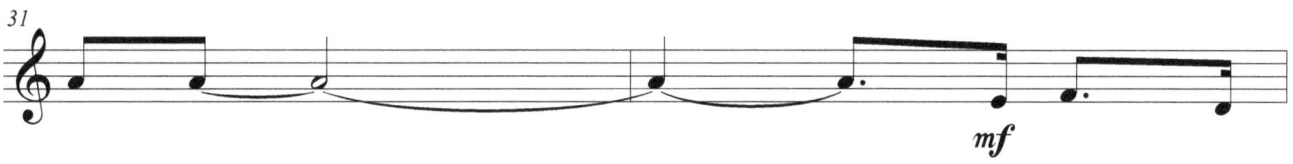
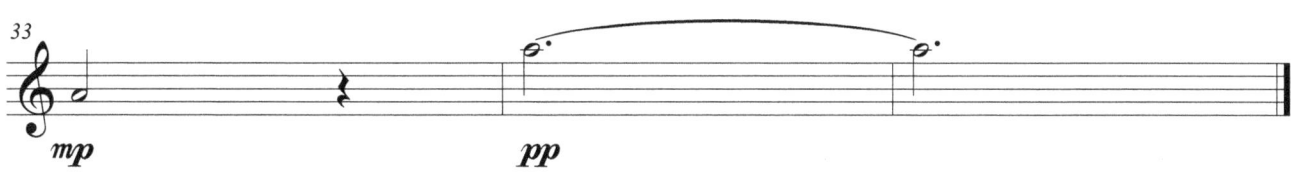

Queen of the Night's Aria

Theme from "The Magic Flute" by W. A. Mozart - 1791

Transcription and arrangement by Antonio Zaccaria - 2015

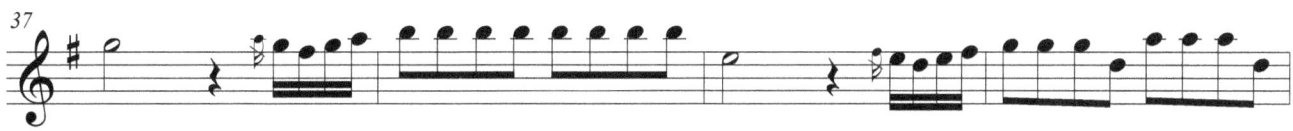

Nessun dorma

Theme form "Turandot" by G. Puccini - 1926

Transcription and arrangement by Antonio Zaccaria - 2015

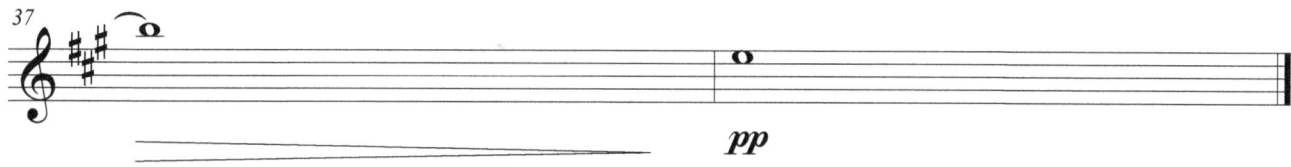

Titolo | Eight opera themes transcribed
and arranged for two guitars and Bb clarinet / flute

Autore | Antonio Zaccaria

ISBN | 978-88-93213-20-2

© Tutti i diritti riservati all'Autore
Nessuna parte di questo libro può
essere riprodotta senza il
preventivo assenso dell'Autore.

Youcanprint Self-Publishing
Via Roma, 73 - 73039 Tricase (LE) - Italy www.youcanprint.it
info@youcanprint.it
Facebook: facebook.com/youcanprint.it Twitter: twitter.com/
youcanprintit

Finito di stampare nel mese di Novembre 2015
per conto di Youcanprint *Self - Publishing*